SPRING ON THE FARM

**Peggy Heeks
and Ralph Whitlock**

Illustrated by Anne Howard

First published in 1985 by
Wayland (Publishers) Ltd
49 Lansdowne Place, Hove
East Sussex BN3 1HF, England

© Copyright 1985 Wayland (Publishers) Ltd

ISBN 0 85078 491 3

Filmset by
Latimer Trend & Company Ltd, Plymouth
Printed in Italy by
G. Canale & C.S.p.A., Turin
Bound in the UK by The Pitman Press, Bath

Contents

Spring is a very busy season for the farmer.
One of his first jobs is to make the fields
ready for planting.
This machine is called a cultivator.
It breaks up the lumps of earth
into fine soil.

When the fields are smooth and level
the farmer sows the seeds of grain crops.
He may use seeds of wheat, barley,
oats, maize, rice or rye.
In the picture the tractors are pulling
combine drills.
These machines sow seeds and put fertilizer
into the soil at the same time.
The fertilizer helps the seeds to grow.

Spring is the time when lambs are born.
Mother sheep are called ewes.
If the weather is cold the mother sheep
are taken indoors to have their lambs.
Each ewe and her lamb have their own pen.
The lamb feeds on its mother's milk.
This ewe has had two lambs.

The grass begins to grow again in spring.
The goodness in the young grass helps
the cows to make plenty of milk for
their new-born calves.
This young calf is drinking milk
from its mother.
Cows make more milk in spring
than at any other time.
The farmer sells the spare milk to dairies
for people to drink.

Spring is the natural time for
chickens to be born.
Free-range hens lay most of their eggs in spring.
They sit on their eggs to keep them warm.
The chicks hatch out after three weeks.

Most hens are now kept indoors in cages.
They live in the warm all the time.
They lay their eggs all the year round.
Their chicks are hatched in incubators.

13

Mother pigs are called sows.
The sows come indoors to have their piglets
so they can keep warm.
This vet is examining a young piglet to
make sure it is fit and healthy.

15

Potatoes are planted at the end of spring.
Then the weather is warmer and
there are no frosts.
Frosts might kill the young plants.
The farmer uses a big machine to
plant potatoes in the fields.

The farmer wants his crops to grow quickly.
Sometimes he sprays fertilizer
on the young plants.
This helps them to grow strong and healthy.
This farmer is spraying chemicals
over his plants.
The chemicals kill pests and germs
that could harm the crops.

Lambs stay with their mothers
all through spring.
They soon learn to feed on grass
instead of milk.
They graze in the fields and eat the fresh grass
that grows in the spring.

21

Cows do not always go into the fields
to eat grass.
Sometimes the farmer cuts fresh grass and
takes it to the cows in their houses.
This way the cows do not waste the grass by
treading on it or dropping their dung on it.
Feeding cows like this is called zero grazing.

The vegetables that have been growing
in the fields all winter are
ready to be eaten in spring.
Leeks, parsnips, turnips and broccoli
are all spring vegetables.
They can live through hard winter frosts.
This farmer is using large machines to
harvest his leeks.

The grass grows quickly in the spring.

The farmer cuts some to make into animal food.

This tractor is pulling a forage harvester.

The forage harvester collects the cut grass.

The grass is pressed down and
covered to keep out the air.

It is used to feed the animals in winter.

Grass kept like this is called silage.

Bees wake up in the spring after
their long winter sleep.
They collect nectar from flowers
to make honey.
Bees carry pollen from flower to flower.
This helps the plants to make their seeds.
Farmers who have orchards like to see
bees at work on their fruit trees.
After the bees have been busy
the farmer will have a good crop of fruit.

Some harmful insects are
born in the spring.
The sheep fly lays its eggs
in sheep's wool.
When maggots hatch from the eggs
they eat the sheep's flesh.
The farmer dips his sheep in disinfectant
to kill the flies and the eggs.

Glossary

Disinfectant Something which kills germs.

Free-range hens Hens that are kept in natural conditions, not in cages.

Incubator A machine for hatching eggs without hens sitting on them.

Maggots Small worms which grow and change into flies.

Nectar A sweet liquid made by flowers which bees use to make honey.

Pen A small area surrounded by fences so that animals can be kept there.

Pollen The yellow powder in flowers which they use to make seeds.

Season One of the four parts of the year (spring, summer, autumn or winter).

Spring The time between the cold winter months and the warmer summer months. In the northern countries of the world spring is in March, April and May. In the southern countries of the world spring is in September, October and November.

Index